VIRTUALBOX

An Ultimate Guide Book on Virtualization with VirtualBox

Copyright©2015 Harry Colvin
All Rights Reserved

Table of contents

Disclaimer

While all attempts have been made to verify the information provided in this book, the author does assume any responsibility for errors, omissions, or contrary interpretations of the subject matter contained within. **The information provided in this book is for educational and entertainment purposes only. The reader is responsible for his or her own actions and the author does not accept any responsibilities for any liabilities or damages, real or perceived, resulting from the use of this information.**

The trademarks that are used are without any consent, and the publication of the trademark is without permission or backing by the trademark owner. All trademarks and brands within this book are for clarifying purposes only and are the owned by the owners themselves, not affiliated with this document.

Introduction

Most computer users are experts in the various operating systems which are available. These include the Windows operating system, Linux, and the Mac OS X. However, they have not been able to run more one operating system in their system simultaneously. Although it is possible for one to install more than one operating system into their computer, it is difficult for them to these operating systems simultaneously. VirtualBox was brought out to solve this problem. With this, you do not have to natively install more than operating systems in your computer. Once you have one operating system installed, may it be Linux, Windows, or Mac OS X, just install the VirtualBox application. This will let you run the rest of the operating systems from it. Any number of operating systems can be installed on the VirtualBox with the only limitation being the memory and speed of your computer. This shows how useful and important the application is. The operating system run on the VirtualBox can either be the desktop or the server version as all are supported.

Chapter 1- Definition

VirtualBoxprovides a platform for a cross-platform virtualization. It can be installed on any of the operating systems which are used by users. However, note that there is a version for each of these operating systems, so you should download the right one for your operating system. With this platform, the capabilities of your computer are extended since it becomes possible for you to run multiple operating systems on the native one. An example is a user who has installed the Windows operating systems on their computer. It is possible for them to use VirtualBox and run other operating systems such as Mac OS X or Linux on this. It also saves you the task of having to install more than one operating systems on your computer, and especially for those whose computers have issues having to do with the storage space. If you need to use the server versions of your operating systems, these can also be installed on VirtualBox. With VirtualBox, the only limitation that can affect you is the disk space and the memory of your computer.

VirtualBox can be used in a wide variety of environments, ranging from the simple desktop system to cloud environments, and it will provide efficient services. Most people are shocked once they create a virtual machine on VirtualBox. This is because the OS installed here runs exactly the same as how it runs when installed natively into the computer. The operating systems which are being run on the VirtualBox can also be run simultaneously, in addition to the natively installed operating system, showing how flexible the system is. The process of creating a virtual machine on VirtualBox is fast and easy, so you should not be worried about this. It will be deeply discussed in this book.

Chapter 2- Installation of VirtualBox

In this chapter, we will discuss the necessary steps to install VirtualBox in a computer. Note that it is possible for you to install VirtualBox on any operating system used in computers, including all the distributions of Linux. We said that there is a version of VirtualBox for the various types and versions of the operating systems.

Installation on Windows

VirtualBox can be installed on Windows. You need to begin by downloading the version of VirtualBox which was developed for the Windows OS. For this case, there is the "*x64*" and the "*x86*," so make sure that you download the right one for yourself.

Once the download completes, you can then begin the installation process. Just double click on the downloaded package. You can also open the command prompt and then enter the following command:

VirtualBox.exe –extract

The above command will extract the downloaded package in a temporary directory in which you will find the MSI files. To begin the installation process, just execute the following command on the same command prompt:

msiexec /iVirtualBox-<version>-MultiArch_<x86|amd64>.msi

Once you run the above command, an installation dialog will be presented to you, where you will be asked to provide the path where the package is to be installed.

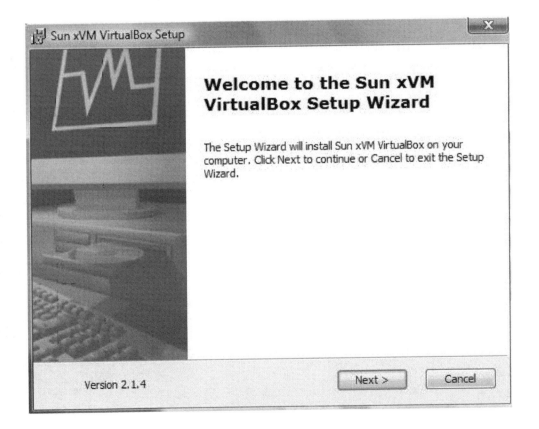

As shown and directed in the installation wizard given above, just click on the *"Next"* button, and the installation process will continue. Just follow the steps since the installation dialog will guide you. Once you have chosen the directory where to install the platform, the installation will continue, and you will be asked to finish the installation process. You will then be done.

Installation on Linux

As we said earlier, it is possible for us to install and run VirtualBox on the various distributions of Linux. You only need to begin by downloading the package for Linux. The current and latest version of VirtualBox is 5.0, so you can choose to download this version in order to enjoy the new and latest features associated with the platform.

If you are running Debian/Ubuntu on your computer, just execute the following command so as to download the package:

sudodpkg   -i   virtualbox-5.0_5.0.0_Ubuntu_raring_i386.deb

Our assumption in the command is that you want to download the 32-bit version of the installation pACKAGE. If you want to download the 64-bit version of the package, then change the 86 to 64 and all will be well. If asked to accept the License, just accept it by clicking on "*Yes,*" otherwise, the process will be aborted. If you need to build the module in a second attempt, just run the following command:

sudorcvboxdrv setup

The installation process will continue, and finally it will complete. A shortcut will be created on the desktop and once you launch it, you will observe the following Window:

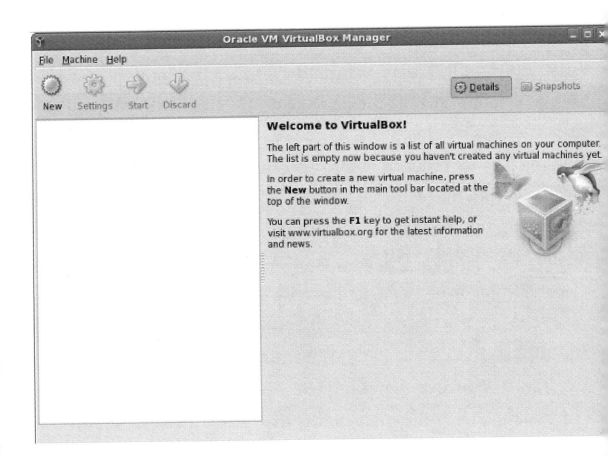

Chapter 3- Creating a New Virtual Machine

Since the installation is complete, we need to create a new virtual machine in the VirtualBox. This virtual machine can be of any operating system. To do this, just follow the steps given below:

1. In the toolbar, identify the *"New"* button and then click on it. A new virtual machine wizard will be presented as shown in the figure below:

2. Click on the button labeled *"Next"* as shown above, and then continue with the installation steps. You will be asked

to provide a name for the virtual name, so provide a name which is related to the kind of OS that you are creating a virtual machine for. You also have to select the type of operating system for the virtual machine.

If you select the right version of the operating system for the virtual machine, then this will help the VirtualBox to apply the default settings for it. If you choose the wrong one, this might make the settings to be incompatible with the virtual machine, meaning that errors will arise.

3. The wizard will also ask you to specify the amount of memory space to be taken by the virtual machine. You can leave this at its default and all will be well.

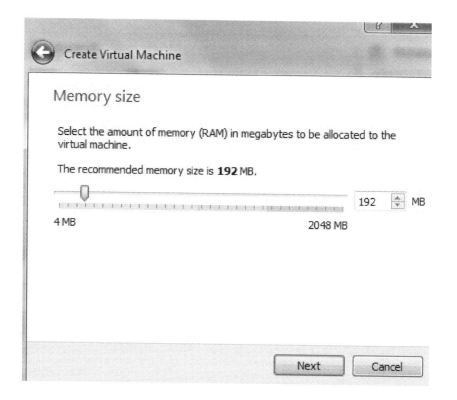

As shown in the above figure, my virtual machine will occupy 192 MB of the space, which is the default setting in my case.

4. The next step will be for the Virtual hard disk. Enable the "*Create new hard disk*" option by checking its check button. The "*Start-up disk*" option should also be enabled by checking its check box. This is shown in the figure given below:

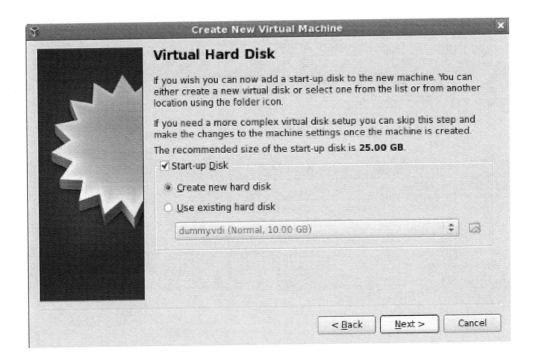

For some versions of VirtualBox, these options will come checked by default. Once done, click on the *"Next"* button.

5. A wizard will then be presented to you. For the type of the image which is to be used, select the VDI (Virtual Disk Image). For the rest of the details, such as the location, accept the default settings.

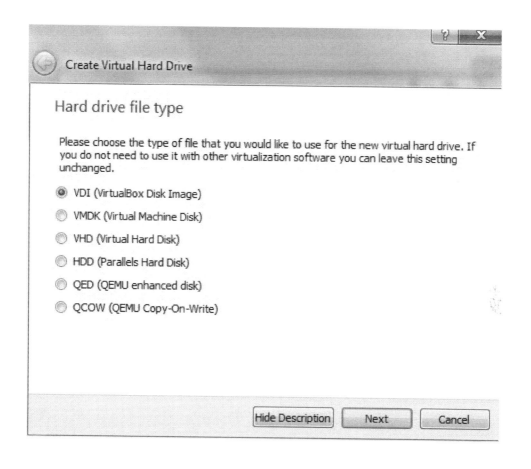

6. Click on the "*Next*" button just shown above. Choose "*Dynamically allocated*" in the next wizard which appears.

Please choose whether the new virtual hard drive file should grow as it is used (dynamically allocated) or if it should be created at its maximum size (fixed size).

A **dynamically allocated** hard drive file will only use space on your physical hard drive as it fills up (up to a maximum **fixed size**), although it will not shrink again automatically when space on it is freed.

A **fixed size** hard drive file may take longer to create on some systems but is often faster to use.

◉ Dynamically allocated

◎ Fixed size

You can then click on the *"Next"* button to continue. In the next wizard, just click on the *"Create"* button. You will be returned to the home window. Check the left side of the window and you will see the name of the virtual machine which you specified. This is shown below:

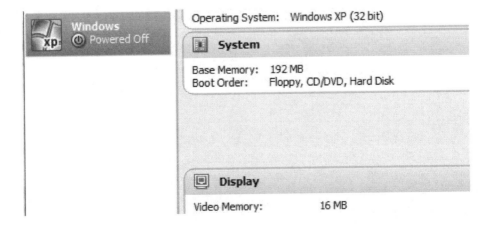

In my case, I created a virtual machine for the Windows operating system and this explains the source of the above output.

7. We now need to finalize the process by choosing the storage media for our virtual machine. The reason is because we are creating an operating system. We need to be sure that our virtual machine will be in a position to access the storage media. To do this, just click or choose the virtual machine on the left side of the above window, and then choose "*Settings*" from the above toolbar. After doing that, you will be presented with the following window:

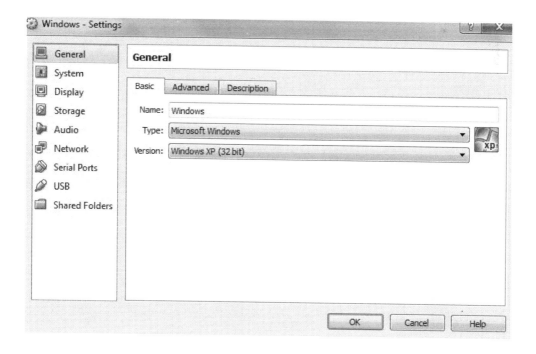

8. On the navigation window displayed on the left, just select *"Storage"*. Under the section written *"Storage Tree"*, select *"Empty"* just below the IDE controller.

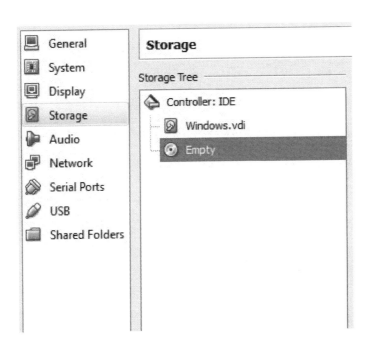

9. Identify the *"CD/DVD"* icon and then click on it. You also have to select the location of the installation media. This can be an ISO file of the operating system which you have downloaded and stored in your system or an ISO file which has been burned on a CD or DVD.

10.   Once you are done, click on the *"Ok"* button so as to apply the changes which you have just made.

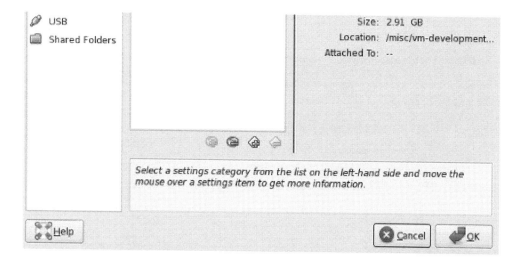

The settings windows will then be closed. If the ISO file was burned to a CD, you can then insert it since we want to get started. We are now ready to start our virtual machine and install our operating system.

11. You can select the virtual machine to the left of the window and then click on the *"Start"* button.This should start the virtual machine. This is shown below:

Once you click on the start button, the processing of launching the virtual machine should begin. The window to be displayed will depend on the kind of operating system that you are creating a virtual machine for. However, you might get some warnings but just ignore them.

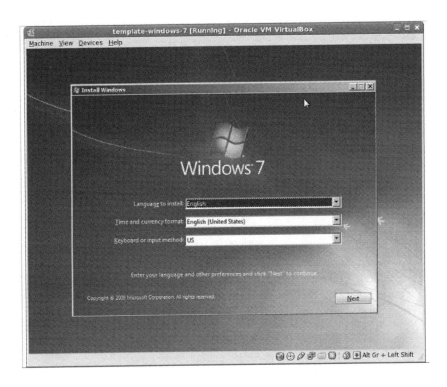

You can then follow the steps as guided in the wizard and you will finally be done. The virtual machine can now be used normally just as you can use your natively installed operating system.

Chapter 4- Installation of Guest additions for the VirtualBox

The guest additions for the VirtualBox consist of the device drivers and the system applications which are responsible for optimization of the operating system so as to offer a better performance and increase the usability. An example of the usability features that we need in this case is the automatic logons. This is the reason why we need to install the guest additions into the virtual machine.

To do this, just open the virtual machine which we created. Click on the *"Device"* menu at the top, and then choose *"Install Guest Additions"*.

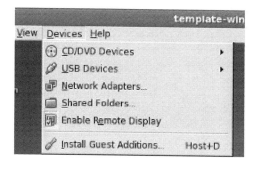

An AutoPlay window will appear which will prompt you to run the program *"VBoxWindowsAdditions.exe."* This is shown below:

Just close the above window. Once you have closed it, the ISO image which was used for installation of Guest Additions will be left inserted in the virtual CD/DVD drive. For us to obtain all the necessary features, we need to install the Guest features from the command prompt.

In our virtual machine, click on the Windows *"Start Menu."* In the search field provided, just type *"run"* and then hit the *"Return"* key. You will be presented with the Run Dialog. In the text field which is visible in the Run Dialog, just type *"D:\VBoxWindowsAdditions.exe /with_autologon"* and again, hit the *"Return"* key.

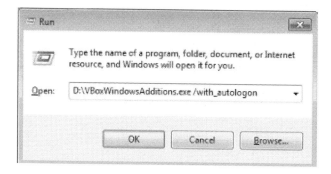

When you are prompted to install the Guest Additions or not, just click on "*Yes,*" and the installation will commence. The setup wizard for installations of Guest Additions in VirtualBox will be displayed as it is shown in the figure given below:

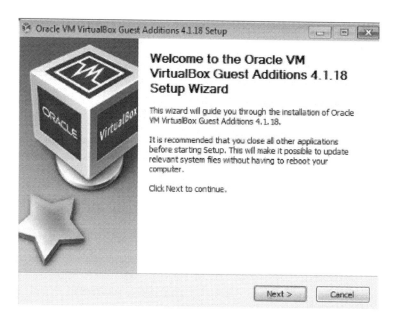

Click on the button labeled "*Next*" as shown in the figure. Any default settings in the next steps should just be accepted. You need not to worry about what they are. Once you see a button labeled "*Install,*" just click on it and this will install the Guest

Additions in your virtual machine. It is possible for a Windows security dialog to appear which will prompt you to do an installation of the device software. This is shown in the figure given below:

If this is the case, just click on the *"Install"* button, and the installation process will continue. The process will continue and after a while, the Guest Additions will be installed on the system. Just enable the option for *"Reboot now,"* and then click on the *"Finish"* button.

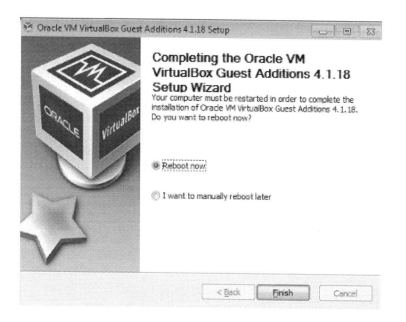

With the wizard shown in the figure, clicking on the *"Finish"* button will restart the system. After the virtual machine is rebooted, just log into it.

Now that you are ready, it is also good for you to make some automated logon work and to connect the computer to a domain. The built-in administrator account needs to be disabled, and the Windows Secure Authentication Sequence needs to be disabled. These can only be achieved by editing the local security policies residing in our virtual machine.

Just open the Windows start menu and then in the search field, type *"run"* and subsequently hit the *"Return"* key. You will be presented with the Run Dialog. In it, just type *"Local Security Policy"* and again, hit the *"Return"* key. A window for Local

Security Policy will be displayed. Click on "*Local Policies,*" and then select "*Security Options.*"

Look for the policy "*Accounts: Administrator account status.*" Double click on this policy, and then choose "*Enabled.*" After that, choose "*Apply.*"

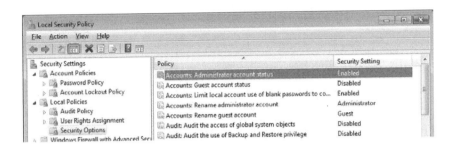

You can then click on the "*Ok*" button. However, ensure that the "*Security Setting*" option for this policy is set to "*Enabled*" before clicking on the "*Ok*" button. This is shown in the above figure.

Once you are okay, look for the policy "*Interactive logon: Do not require CTRL + ALT + DEL.*" Double click on this policy, and then choose "*Enable.*" Select Apply, and then click on the "*Ok*" button. In the column for the "*Security Option,*" make sure that this is shown to be "*Enabled*" before clicking on the "*Ok*" button, which will finalize everything. This is shown in the figure given below:

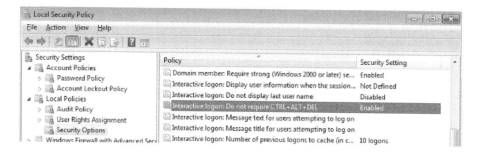

The Local Security Policy window should then be closed. We now want to create the password for the local Administrator account which is built-in. Open the Control Panel for the Windows, and then click on *"User Accounts."* Select *"Administrator user"* and then set a password for it. You should then verify whether this administrator account is working. To do this, you just have to log out of the Windows and then log in again, but as the Administrator user. If you login in successfully, then know that you are well set.

Just use the Windows menu to shut down the virtual machine.

Note that it is also possible for you to use the VirtualBox menu so as to shut down the virtual machine. If this is the case or what you want to do, then make sure that the option *"elect the ACPI shutdown (send the shutdown signal)"* is selected. With this option enabled, the state of the virtual machine will be well preserved, and it will be shut down in the normal way. If you enable the option *"Close (power off the machine),"* the state of the virtual machine will not be preserved, and the kind of shutdown used will not be a normal one. With this, the virtual machine can get damaged.

At this moment, your machine can be used to provide a template in which desktops can be created.

Chapter 5- How to create the Desktops

In the Oracle virtual Disk Image, we group desktops together, depending on their characteristics to make the task of managing these easy. A pool must first be created, to where a virtual machine will be imported for provision of a template for the purpose of cloning. We then have to enable the cloning, so as to fill the clone with desktops. Users are then assigned to the clone, and they will be in a position to access the desktops.

Creation of a Pool

For you to create a pool, begin by opening the Oracle VDI Manager. On the left section, just select the *"Pools"* option. You should then choose your company, that is, the one which you had just created. With pools, they should only be linked to companies. This will make it possible for users to access the authorized desktops and not the wrong ones.

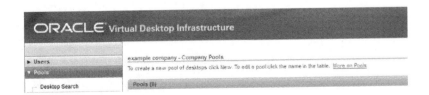

Click on the button written *"New"* in the *"Pools"* table. A wizard named *"New Pool"* will be displayed. Moves through the various steps of this wizard by just clicking on the *"Next"* button.Once you reach the step *"Select Pool Type,"* just select the desktop provided which you had just created. This should be visible from the drop-down list. In the case of the pool type, select *"Dynamic Pool"* for this.This is shown in the figure given below:

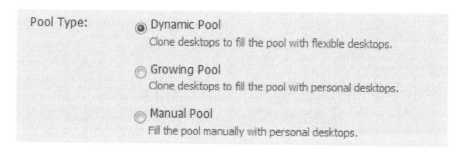

The Desktop Provider is responsible for linking the pool to the necessary virtualization resources which will help you to run the desktops. The Pool Type settings are just for helping you to easily create the pool of your choice. However, these configurations can be changed later.

A window will appear for you to select the template. From the drop down list, ensure that the option *"(None)"* is selected. In the *"System Preparation"* option, *"none"* should also be the selected choice. This is shown in the figure given below:

Select a template for the new pool and specify the System Preparation.

Template: (None) ▼
System Preparation: none   ▼

If a template had been used in another pool, then this step will give you choice of selecting it. The system preparation and the template settings can then be configured later, after configuration of cloning for the pool.

The next step will be for configuring the size of the pool. You leave this to the default size for the option *"Preferred Size."* The option for the *"Enable Automatic Cloning"* should also not be checked. This is shown in the figure given below:

Specify the average number of necessary desktops for the pool.

Preferred Size: 10
                 The desired number of desktops in the pool

Cloning: ☐ Enable Automatic Cloning
                 If a template is available, cloning will start immediately.

The next step will be defining the name for the pool. Identify the field for *"Name"* and then provide the appropriate name for the pool. You can choose any name, but in most cases, users choose to use the name of the operating system they have used or the department which will use the desktops. Comments can also be provided, though it is optional. This is shown in the figure given below:

The final step will be for doing the review of the pool. Just identify the button labeled"*Finish,*" and then click on it. This will definitely create the pool. The wizard will also be closed. A message, indicating whether or not the pool was created will be displayed on the page of the company. The pool will also be part of the list in the pools table. This is shown in the figure given below:

The above figure shows that the pool was successfully created. In case yours fails, try to repeat the steps and all will be well.

Chapter 6- How to import a Template into the Pool

The purpose of the template is to be used for cloning the desktops. For this to happen, we have to clone it into the pool.

In the Pools table for the company, move to the column named "*Name,*" and then click on the name of the pool that you created. The tab for "*Summary*" will be displayed. Click on the tab named "*Template.*" The page for the Pool Template will be displayed.

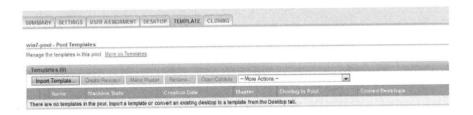

In the "*Templates*" table shown above, just click on the button labeled "*Import Template.*" This is located to the left side of the above window. The window for importing the template will be displayed. On the tab named "*Folder,*" it is possible for us to import a template from the folder "*/var/tmp*" which is located on the host, or from the NFS share located on the host or just another host. On the tab designated "*Hypervisor,*" you can directly import the template from the installation of the VirtualBox on the host or another host.

If the disk image and the virtual machine settings file had been copied to the "/var/tmp" folder, click on the button labeled "*Select folder.*" If the loading is not done automatically, just move to the drop down list, and then select the disk image or the settings file. However, the option "*Delete original desktop after successful import*" should not be selected.

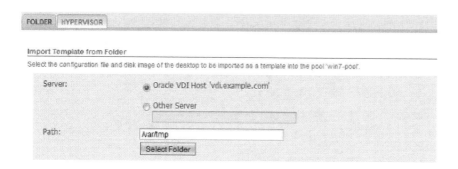

If you correctly followed and adhered to the steps which we discussed for importation of an existing virtual machine into the VirtualBox, then just click on the tab written "*Hypervisor*" as shown in the above figure.The template can then be selected from the list of the available desktops in the host. However, make sure that the option "*Delete original desktop after successful import*" is not selected. This is shown in the figure given below:

☐ Delete original desktop after successful import

The import process can take several minutes.

However, it is possible that you might need to import the desktops individually into the pool other than the template itself. The steps are just similar to what we have done,but in this case, you will have to perform them in the tab labeled *"Desktop."*

To start the importation of the template, just click on the button labeled *"Ok."*The window for importation of the template will be closed, and you will see a message on the tab named *"Template"* which will tell you that the template was imported. This is shown in the figure given below:

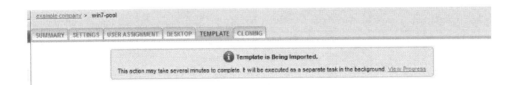

Most actions users perform in the Oracle VDI usually create jobs whose execution will be done in the background. This means that as they are executed, we can continue to perform some other tasks. The template can then be imported into one of the actions which result into a job. In the Oracle VDI Manager, move to the top-right corner and then identify the *"Jobs Running"* link. You will see the summary of jobs which are currently running displayed on a window as shown below:

The jobs which are running at the moment will be displayed on the above window. The details and summary of the job will be given. After the process of importing the template completes, the template will be displayed in the "*templates*" table located in the tab labeled "*Template.*"Just click on the Arrowhead,which is next to this template in the column labeled "*Name.*" You will then realize that the first revision of the template has been automatically created. It will also be marked as the master revision of the template.

During the cloning process, the desktops are just created from the revisions. The purpose of the revision is just to save the current state of the virtual machine, for example, when shutting it down so that it can pick from there the next time it is started. Changes to the template can be made at any time. A good example of this is when you want to install a particular software program, and then test whether it is running effectively or not. Once you find it working effectively or as you expected, a new revision can then be created and then made the master revision. Cloning of the new desktops can then be done by use of this template. In case problems with the revision are discovered later, it is also possible for you to switch to the previous one andthen make it the master.

Changes to the template can also be made from within the Oracle VDI Manager. This can be done by selecting the template, and then clicking on the button written *"Open Console."*A Console Page will be shown. From this page, you can start, stop, and also establish a connection to the virtual machine just in the same way that we did in the Oracle VM VirtualBox Manager.

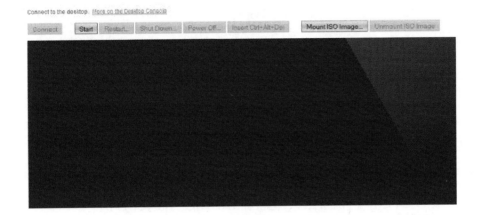

Chapter 7- How to set up the Cloning

We now need to set up the cloning. Once this has been set up, the filling of the pool with the desktops which we require will be done automatically. A configuration will also need to be done so that the desktops which we have cloned will be in a position to join the Windows domain.

Just identify the tab labeled *"Cloning"* and then click on it. This is shown in the figure given below:

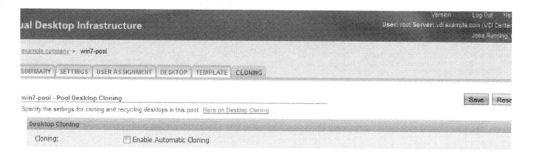

In the group for *"Desktop Cloning,"* select the option labeled *"Enable Automatic Cloning."* You can also change the name contained in the *"Name Pattern."* This is responsible for generation of the name for the virtual machine which has been cloned. This will also be the computer's name used for registration with the Windows domain.

Desktop Cloning	
Cloning:	☑ Enable Automatic Cloning

In the Metrics group for the cloning, it will be possible for you to configure the number of desktops that you need in the pool. This is shown below:

- Preferred Size- This is the number of desktops that the pool has in normal circumstances. This is set to two.

- Maximum Size- this is the maximum number of desktops that the pool can have. It is set to three.

- Free Desktops and Production Priority-do not interfere with these, but just leave them at their default setting.

In most cases, it is highly recommended that you start with a small pool. The reason for this is because you can increase its size in the future once you are sure that it works in the way that you expected it to. When the process of cloning begins, the Oracle VDI Manager will do it by use of the number of desktops that you had set. The desktops in the pool will definitely get used, and if this is the case, the Oracle VDI will use the free desktops setting so as to know whether there is a need for more desktops to be cloned. However, you need to note that the number of the desktops which have been used in the pool will never exceed the maximum number which you had specified or set. When the desktops are not being used, they will be reduced to the size which is preferred. Note that this is automatically done on your behalf.

You can then identify the group *"Cloned Desktops"* and then select the template which you just imported into the pool. This can be found in the provided drop down list. However, it doesn't have to be in the pool, but it can just be located in another pool but for the same company, which is okay.

For the cloned desktops to be deployed from the template, we need to correctly prepare our system. For this purpose, we can choose to use either FastPrep (which is an Oracle VDI Fast preparation tool) or SysPrep (which is a Microsoft Windows System Preparation tool). With the SyssPrep, additional preparations will have to be done to the template. With FastPrep, the preparation can be done faster since no additional preparations have to be done to the template. With SysPrep, Windows deployment tools have to be installed to the template and then remove the unique information by running the program. With FastPrep, the computer name is simply updated rather than being removed.

In the group for the *"Cloned Desktops,"* just select *"Create,"* which is located next to the *"System Preparation."* The window for the *"Create System Preparation File"* will be displayed.

In the drop down list which is provided, select *"Oracle VDI Fast Preparation."* The operating system used in your template should also be matched correctly, otherwise, errors might arise. For the rest of the details, provide the necessary ones.

Create System Preparation File
Specify the system preparation. Any existing preparation file will be overwritten.

System Preparation: Oracle VDI Fast Preparation for Windows Vista or Windows 7 ▾

Once you are through with the details, just click on the *"Ok"* button, and this will finish the specification of FastPrep. The window for *"Create System preparation File"* will be closed. A message will then be displayed, and it will tell that the preparation of SysPrep was done successfully.

The *"Machine State"* in the Cloned Desktop Group can be used for specification of the state that the desktop virtual machines will be at immediately after the cloning has been done. From the drop down list which is provided, just select "*Running.*"Note that once you have shut down the virtual machines, no computer resources will be consumed. The setting "*Available Running Desktops*" can be used for specification of desktops that the Oracle VDI can keep running once the user has logged in. If the desktops are set to running, then it will be good for the sake of saving time, since the users will not have to wait for the VM (Virtual Machine) to boot. This is shown in the figure given below:

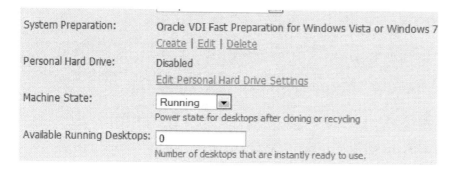

The settings in the group "*Desktop recycling*" will determine what happens to our desktops when no one is using them. When any of the desktops is not being used, the Oracle VDI recycles them. The "*Policy*" setting is responsible for controlling a desktop which has been recycled, and the following are some of the actions which can be taken:

- Reset to Snapshot- in this case, the desktop will be powered off, and then it will be reset to the snapshot which was taken after cloning of the desktop was done.

- Reuse Desktop- a reuse of the desktop is done and then it is kept in its current state.

- Delete Desktop- a delete of the desktop is done, and if it is found that there are not enough desktops for the pool, then a new one will be cloned from the template.

Notice that we are using the *"Idle Timeout."*In this case, if a desktop is unused before this period expires, then the desktop will be recycled. If you need the process of recycling of the desktop to be done quickly, then you should set the parameter Idle Timeout to be a number which is small, such as three minutes. This is shown in the figure given below:

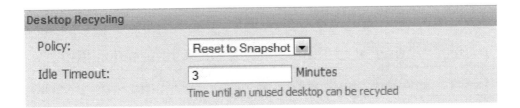

Once done, click on the button labeled *"Save."*A message showing that the configuration has been applied will be displayed. After a short while, the running jobs will be shown on the top-right corner. This is shown in the figure given below:

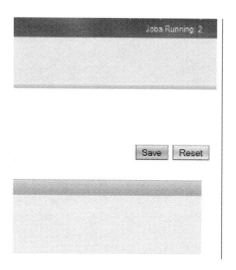

Open the Oracle VDI Manager and then at the top right corner of the same, click on the link labeled"*Jobs Running.*"A window showing the summary of the running jobs will be displayed. The running jobs should be made up by the desktops which have been added or cloned to the pool.

Close the window for the summary of the jobs, and then click on the tab labeled "*Desktop.*"When the process of cloning of the desktops is being done, these are listed in the Desktops table. Initially, their state will be shown to be reserved. This is a clear indication that the Oracle VDI, which in this case is the FastPrep, is performing some work on the desktop. The status of the virtual machine can change, depending on what you selected at the tab for "*Cloning.*"However, the column for "*Desktop state*" will show that the desktops which you created have been cloned. This is shown in the figure given below:

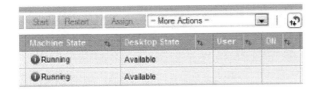

Chapter 8- How to assign users to the Desktops

We now need to make users be in a position to access the desktops in the pool. This can be done by assigning users to the pool.

In the pool, click on the tab labeled *"User Assignment."*This is shown in the figure given below:

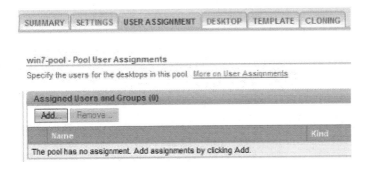

In the table labeled *"Assigned Users and Groups,"* click on the button labled *"Add."*A window named *"Assign Pool"* will be displayed. This is shown in the figure given below:

In Oracle VDI, there are numerous ways how users can be assigned to the pool. However, it is highly recommended that you use the method of searching for the directory containing users and groups. The reason is because assignment of users contained in the group to the pool is the most efficient method. This will mean that the users in the group have been indirectly assigned to the pool. If the membership of the group is changed in the future, then users who are allowed to access the pool will also be updated or changed.

If you need to search the directory for a user, just select the "*User or Group*" option. In the field labeled "*Search Users and Groups,*" just enter the name of the user or the group, and then begin the search process by clicking on the button labeled "*Search.*"

Note that this search is case insensitive, so you need not to be worried about this. The search results, which will be limited to the first 100 found users or groups will then be displayed or shown in a table.

However, if you need to make your work much easier and efficient, it is recommended that you should use the group which is built-in. With this, any user who is located in the directory for the user will be able to access the desktops contained in the pool. To use this option, rather than selecting the option shown in the above figure, just select the "Custom Group" one. Just below this, you will see the option "Any User" with a check box. Just select this by enabling its check box. This is shown in the figure given below:

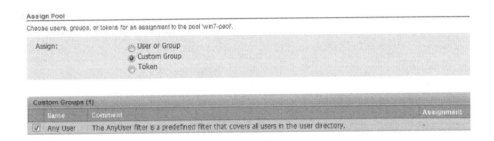

You can then click on the button labeled "Ok." The window for "Assign Pool" will then be closed. A success message showing that the assignment was added will be displayed. This is shown in the figure given below:

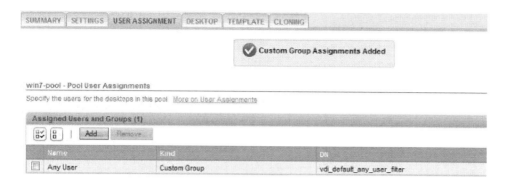

Alternatively, one can use the smart card array functionality which is provided by the Sun Array environment for assignment of users to a particular pool. With Oracle VDI, the smart cards will be referred to as the tokens. If these tokens are assigned to the pool, the users will be able to use the Sun Array client and perform some authentication on the Oracle VDI, which will allow them to access the desktops.

You might also need to assign each of the individual desktops to a particular user. This can be done from the tab for "*Desktop*" in the pool. However, this will mean that the desktop will have been converted to a personal one, that is, for a single user rather than being a flexible one which can be accessed by any user in the pool. However, it is highly recommended that one should use a flexible desktop,since the work of management of desktops will become much easier. Most of the tasks will be done automatically in bulk. In the case of the personal desktop, the management has to be done individually and manually for each of the available desktops.

Chapter 9- Establishing a connection to the Desktop

Now that everything has been set up, we need to establish a connection to the desktop which is contained in the pool. You just have to log into the Oracle VDI from where you will be able to access the desktop. The Oracle Virtual desktop client needs to be started. On the screen for the Connect Virtual Desktop Client, provide the DNS name which is fully qualified which is associated to the Oracle VDI host. This should be in the server field. Once you are done, just click on the *"Connect"* button.

Desktop Login

After some time, the Windows desktop will be displayed. You will then be logged into the Windows desktop automatically. It is possible that a message telling you that preparation of the desktop is being done will be displayed. If this happens, just be patient and wait for the process to complete. What happens is the preparation of how the folders will be displayed on the desktop. Once this is done or completed, the usage of the desktop can be used as normal.

It is possible that your username is assigned to more than one desktop. In this case, a desktop selector will be presented to you from which you will be in a position to select the one that you need to use. This screen will be as follows:

Available Desktops

You are logged in as 'awalker'.

A desktop in pool ubuntu-pool
A desktop in pool win7-pool

Connect	Logout

ℹ Select a desktop to connect.

The above figure shows that the username of the person trying to log into the system is assigned to two desktops. It also possible for you to connect to more than one desktop simultaneously.However, support for multiple monitors must have been configured.

Once you are logged into the desktop, open the Windows Control Panel and then choose *"System and Security."*Select *"System."*Check for the information about the desktop. The information should tell that the computer has been connected to a domain, and the name of the computer should be the name of the desktop which is contained in the pool. The name of the user should be shown on the start menu of the Windows, so you can check for this. The user name should be the correct one.

View basic information about your computer

Windows edition

Windows 7 Enterprise

Copyright © 2009 Microsoft Corporation. All rights reserved.

Service Pack 1

System

Rating:	**1.0** Your Windows Experience Index needs to be refreshed
Processor:	Intel(R) Xeon(R) CPU X5472 @ 3.00GHz 3.00 GHz
Installed memory (RAM):	2.00 GB
System type:	64-bit Operating System
Pen and Touch:	No Pen or Touch Input is available for this Display

Chapter 10- Management of the Desktops

You should learn how the desktops contained in a pool can be managed.

Note that the Oracle VDI can manage the desktops for you automatically. For this to happen, the pools must be configured to use clone for production of flexible desktops. If you watch and then understand the life cycle of a desktop, then it will be better for you as you will understand what it entails to administer it.

Log into your Windows and the open the Oracle VDI Manager. Click on the tab labeled *"Desktop."*In the Desktops table, observe the *"Desktop state"*column, and you will notice that the state of one of these desktops is *"Used."*You will also realize that the name of the user who is currently using the desktop is shown. This is shown in the figure given below:

Machine State	Desktop State
Running	Used
Running	Available

You can then return to the desktop.and log out of your Windows. To do this, just use the normal method that you use to log out in Windows. Once you log out of your Windows, the logging out of the Oracle VDI should be done automatically. Just navigate to the Oracle VDI Manager, and then open the tab labeled *"Desktop,"* but for the pool. Wait for some time, and you will notice that the state of the desktop will be changed to *"Idle."*However, the user will still be assigned to this desktop.

Since the desktop is a flexible one, the assignment of a user to it is a temporary one. If the same user performs a login during this idle timeout, they will be reconnected to the same desktop. If the idle timeout expires during the idle period, the assignment of the user to the desktop is removed, and then the desktop is recycled. The state of this desktop will then be changed to *"Available."*This means that any user can be assigned to this desktop. This is shown in the figure given below:

Machine State	Desktop State	User	DH
⏻ Running	Available		
⏻ Running	Available		

Manual actions can also be performed on any of the desktops from the *"Desktop"* tab of the pool. From the Desktop table, select a desktop and then click on the drop down list labeled *"More Actions."*This is shown in the figure given below:

Identify a desktop whose state is shown as "*Available*," and then from the drop down list, select "*Delete Desktop.*"After a short while, you will notice that a new cloning job will be started. The reason for this is because cloning for our pool is enabled and that the current number of desktops is still less than the maximum number which we have configured.

Move to the Desktop table and in the column for the "*Name*," click on one of the desktops. The summary page for the desktop will be displayed. The page or the window will present the information about the desktop and the virtual machine in detail.

Chapter 11- Set up a shared folder

A shared folder in VirtualBox is one of the features which are introduced by the installing of the Guest Additions. After installing this, you can go ahead and set up a shared folder in the host.

To set up this, just navigate to the VirtualBox menu and then click on "*Devices -> Shared Folder..*

Now from the host machine, select a folder which you need to share with the guest machine. This procedure is shown in the figure given below:

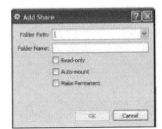

Once you are done, you can then mount the shared folder on the guest machine. In my case, the guest machine is running Linux, specifically Fedora. The host machine is running Windows. You have to create a folder in which the shared folder in which the mounting of the shared folder will be done. The following command can be used for this purpose:

mkdirmyfolder-host

The folder can then be mounted on the shared folder "*myfolder-host.*" This can be done by use of the command given below:

mount -t vboxsfmyfolder-host

An auto-mount can also be done on each boot. If you need to do this, just add the above command to the file "*/etc/rc.local*" or in any other file which is executed after the end of a successful boot process.

Chapter 12- Enabling logging for the .MSI host installer of VirtualBox

For an in-depth analysis, two logs are needed, which are the driver installation log and the installer log of the Windows itself. In case you are asked for these, kindly provide them.

Performing a Clean up

In case installation problems are experienced on Windows, the Microsoft Installer CleanUp utility might have to be run. This tool is available online for a free download, so you can download and then run it. The VirtualBox will not be uninstalled but the problems experienced during the previous installation procedure will be cleaned up.

The Installer Log

Activating it automatically

During the installation of VirtualBox for Windows, one can enable the login. To do this, the installer executable should be started with the parameter "-l". To do this, just launch the Windows command prompt, and then use it to navigate to the directory where the executable of the installer has been stored. In the directory, just run the following command:

VirtualBox-<the-version>-Win.exe -l

The parameter *"the-version"* should be substituted with the version of the installer which you have downloaded.

<u>Doing a manual activation</u>

If you need to manually enable logging persistently, follow the steps given below:

1. Click on the *"Start"* and then choose *"Run."*

2. The Run Dialog will appear. In its search field, enter *"regedit.exe,"* and then hit the *"Return"* key.

3. In the left pane, just navigate to the *"HKEY_LOCAL_MACHINE\Software\Policies\Microsoft\Windows\Installer"* key. If this key is not found, then just create it.

4. Right click on the right pane of the window, choose *"New,"* and then select the *"String value."*

5. The name of the value should be *"Logging."*

6. On the newly created Logging, just double click on it. The value for this should then be set to *"voicewarmupx."*

7. The *"regedit.exe"* can then be closed.

Retrieving the Log files

Once you complete the above steps, the host installer for VirtualBox should produce a log which should start with *"MSI"*in the temporary directory the next time the installer is started.

If you are running Windows XP 32-bit, retrieve this directory by navigating to the following:

C:\Documents and Settings\<Your Username>\Local Settings\Temp

If you are running Windows 7, Windows Vista, or Windows XP 64 bit, find this directory in the following location:
C:\Users\<Your Username>\AppData\Local\Temp

The most recent one should be picked, so make sure that you use date as the criteria for picking these.

The Log for Installing Drivers

Logging in the registry can be enabled in the key:
HKEY_LOCAL_MACHINE\Software\Microsoft\Windo ws\CurrentVersion\Setup

You then need to create or set a value named *"LogLevel"*of type *"DWORD"*and then set it to *"4800FFFF"* which is a hexadecimal value.With this set up, the logging of the driver will be verbose.

In the directory "C:\Windows"or in "C:\Windows\Inf," you will find the following log files:

- setupapi.log

- setupapi.app.log \

- setupapi.dev.log

However, it is good for you to ensure that only the information that you need about the VirtualBox is contained in these logs. This is why it is recommended that you rename or even delete these log files before the installation of the VirtualBox is done. Once the VirtualBox installer has been run, these log files should be attached to the bug report in a zipped or RAR format.

Conclusion

It can be concluded that the VirtualBox is a very useful and important application. With the VirtualBox, one can run numerous applications simultaneously in a single computer. The platform supports numerous operating systems which are normally used by users, including Windows, Mac OS X, and the various distributions of Linux. Note that while downloading VirtualBox for your computer, you must identify the correct version since it comes in different versions, that is, for Windows, Linux, and Mac OS X.

In these operating systems, the VirtualBox also comes in different versions for each of them. For example, for Linux and Windows, there are versions for 32 and 64 bits in each. The uses of the VirtualBox are wide, ranging from the single desktop to the cloud environments. In these cases, users have noticed how useful the VirtualBox is. Of course, you cannot install more than two operating systems natively into your computer. This is because of the storage and the speed limitations. However, this is not the casewith the VirtualBox, as one can run multiple operating system simultaneously. Even if you have installed two operating systems in your computer, it is impossible for you to run them simultaneously. The VirtualBox solves this problem.

The installation of the VirtualBox on the different operating systems is different. In Windows, the installation is simple and very direct, as one is guided by the installation wizard. In Linux, one can use the terminal so as to download, extract, and then install the package. Once you have installed the VirtualBox, you can then get to the process of creating your virtual machine. In the case of the name of the virtual machine, choose the name of the operating system which is to be used for creation of the virtual machine so that its default settings can be applied. If you fail to do this, the process can result in errors.

Made in the USA
Middletown, DE
02 December 2016